FANTASTIC
FARM MACHINES

CULTIVATORS

By S. M. Maimone

Gareth Stevens
PUBLISHING

Please visit our website, www.garethstevens.com. For a free color catalog of all our high-quality books, call toll free 1-800-542-2595 or fax 1-877-542-2596.

Library of Congress Cataloging-in-Publication Data

Names: Maimone, S. M. (Sofia Maxwell), 1978- author.
Title: Cultivators / S.M. Maimone.
Other titles: Fantastic farm machines.
Description: New York : Gareth Stevens Publishing, [2016] | Series: Fantastic
  farm machines | Includes index.
Identifiers: LCCN 2016000744 | ISBN 9781482445893 (pbk.) | ISBN 9781482445824
(library bound) | ISBN 9781482445701 (6 pack)
Subjects: LCSH: Cultivators–Juvenile literature. | Agricultural
  machinery–Juvenile literature.
Classification: LCC S683 .M325 2016 | DDC 631.5/1–dc23
LC record available at http://lccn.loc.gov/2016000744

Published in 2017 by
Gareth Stevens Publishing
111 East 14th Street, Suite 349
New York, NY 10003

Designer: Sarah Liddell
Editor: Therese Shea

Photo credits: Cover, p. 1 Chukov/Shutterstock.com; spread background texture used throughout LongQuattro/Shutterstock.com; p. 5 Larisa Lofitskaya/Shutterstock.com; p. 7 Marowski28/Shutterstock.com; p. 9 Yuji Sakai/DigitalVision/Getty Images; p. 11 LianeM/Shutterstock.com; p. 13 Eric Schaal/Contributor/The LIFE Images Collection/Getty Images; p. 15 oticki/Shutterstock.com; p. 17 Gerard Koudenburg/ Shutterstock.com; p. 19 mertcan/Shutterstock.com; p. 21 servantes/Shutterstock.com.

Printed in the United States of America

CPSIA compliance information: Batch #CS16GS: For further information contact Gareth Stevens, New York, New York at 1-800-542-2595.

CONTENTS

Boldface words appear in the glossary.

Seed, Soil, Sunlight

Have you ever grown a plant? First, you put a seed in soil. Then, you water it. Finally, you make sure the plant gets sunlight. Farmers do all these things and more when growing crops. They may use big machines to help them.

Cultivating for Crops

Farmers need their fields to be the healthiest they can be to grow the best crops. This often means they need to till the soil. "Tilling" means breaking up the soil. Another word for tilling is "cultivating."

There are several reasons for cultivating soil. One is that mixing up soil allows air into it. This lets **nutrients** and water move more easily through soil. It also allows plant roots to reach these important things more easily.

Cultivating soil is also a way to tear up weeds that have taken root in soil. Weeds suck up the nutrients and water in soil, leaving less for crops. They also take up space that crops need to spread and grow.

11

Cultivators, Past and Present

On large farms, farmers use machines called cultivators to till the soil. The first cultivators were pulled by horses. When farmers began to drive tractors, they used those to pull their cultivators. Mixing soil and weeding became easier.

Today's cultivators are often mounted on or dragged behind a tractor. Some are self-propelled, which means they have their own **engine**. Some are just a few feet wide, while others are as wide as 80 feet (24 m)!

Kinds of Cultivators

A field cultivator is used just before crops are planted. It's made up of a metal frame, wheels, and many **shanks** that do the work of digging and mixing the earth. Here's a field cultivator before it's lowered onto a field.

field cultivator

shanks

17

Row crop cultivators are used to stop weeds from growing between rows of crops. Parts called **sweeps** cut weeds out of the ground. The sweeps can be moved as needed, so they fit among the crops.

sweeps

row crop cultivator

19

Farming for the Future

Each year, **engineers** come up with new and better cultivators as well as other kinds of farming **equipment**. The equipment makes farming easier and more **efficient**. What kinds of farm machines would you want to use?

GLOSSARY

efficient: able to operate well without waste

engine: a machine that makes power

engineer: someone who plans and builds machines

equipment: tools, clothing, and other objects needed for a job

nutrient: something a living thing needs to grow and stay alive

shank: a long, narrow part of something

sweep: in farming, a V-shaped blade that cuts weeds out of the ground

FARM INFORMATION

BOOKS

Arlon, Penelope, and Tory Gordon-Harris. *Farm*. New York, NY: Scholastic, 2012.

Bodden, Valerie. *A Farming Town*. Mankato, MN: Creative Education, 2008.

Mayer, Cassie. *Farming*. Chicago, IL: Heinemann Library, 2007.

WEBSITES

Farm Equipment List
farmingequipmentcanada.com
Take a look at this list of farm machines, and read what they do.

How Plants Grow
www.sciencekids.co.nz/gamesactivities/plantsgrow.html
Play a game to make a plant grow.

INDEX